Hamlyn Hobby Horses
PRINTING

by Harvey Daniels

illustrated by Ron Brown

prints supplied by Harvey Daniels

photographs by Philip James

HAMLYN
London · New York · Sydney · Toronto

Also in the
Hamlyn Hobby Horse series
Collecting

The publishers wish to thank the following people and organisations
for their help with preparing some of the prints in this book:

Brighton Polytechnic, Printmaking Service Unit
Balfour Middle School, Brighton
Ann d'Arcy Hughes
Martin Rogers
Jane Smith
Judy Stapleton

Published 1974 by The Hamlyn Publishing Group Limited
London · New York · Sydney · Toronto
Astronaut House, Feltham, Middlesex, England
© Copyright 1974 The Hamlyn Publishing Group Limited
ISBN 0 600 34448 7
Filmset by Tradespools Ltd., Frome, Somerset
Printed in Spain by Mateu-Cromo, S.A.

CONTENTS

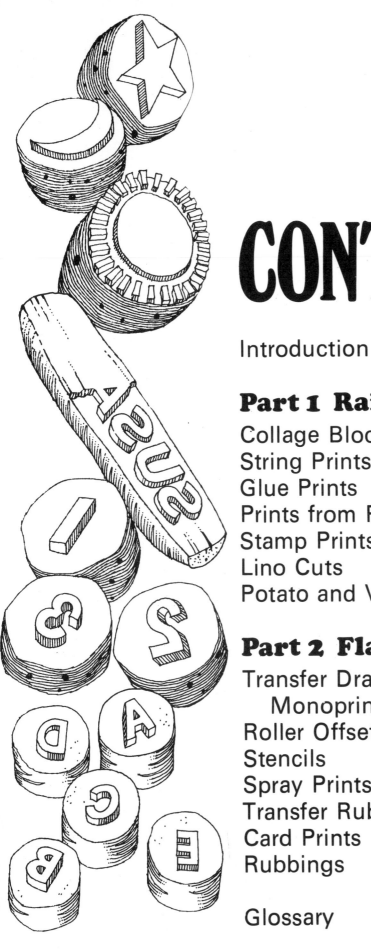

Introduction   8

Part 1 Raised or Relief Printing
Collage Blocks   10
String Prints   16
Glue Prints   23
Prints from Found Objects   26
Stamp Prints   29
Lino Cuts   33
Potato and Vegetable Prints   38

Part 2 Flat Surface Printing
Transfer Drawing and
    Monoprinting   43
Roller Offset   47
Stencils   51
Spray Prints   57
Transfer Rubbing   61
Card Prints   65
Rubbings   70

Glossary   76

Introduction

There is no limit to the variety of exciting things that can be produced by anyone using one of the many techniques of printing. As you will see from this book, two people may make very different things, using the same method.

This book is divided in two parts and covers the main processes of printing. One type of process is *flat*, for example stencilling, roller offset and transfer drawing. The other type of process is *raised,* where the printing is done from the top surface of an object, as in lino cutting, glue prints and potato prints.

Most printing involves certain simple basic materials and equipment such as printing inks and paper. Some of the methods call for the use of rollers made of rubber or gelatine; the larger these are, the better.

Printing inks are available in tins or tubes. Tubes usually hold a smaller quantity of ink than tins, so work out cheaper if you want to buy several different colours. However, it is sensible to buy basic colours, such as white, in larger quantities. It is easier to look after ink in tubes because the colours do not get mixed up with each other; also, ink does not dry in tubes, as long as the caps are replaced after use.

These printing inks are either *water based* or *oil based*. Generally, the oil based ones give the sharpest effect, but they tend to be more difficult to clean off equipment and hands; and clothing too, if an apron is not worn. If you intended to print on fabrics, it would be advisable to buy special fabric-printing colours which do not run or fade and can be washed without the inks cracking.

A kitchen palette knife is the best kind for mixing inks but other flexible knives may be used.

Most objects can be printed, but it is sometimes difficult to decide how to develop ideas. This book should suggest some ideas to you and indicate how they could possibly be carried out, but there are always alternative methods and these would produce very different printed results.

The novice printmaker should soon be able to adapt the ideas in this book for his personal use. Through experience and inventiveness the printmaker can enjoy the satisfaction of producing his own completely original book jackets, record covers, curtains and clothing.

Look in your local library for books on the work of the Spanish artist, Picasso or the French artist, Matisse. Both of these used many of the printing methods which are described in this book.

Many of these chapters overlap and of course it is always possible to combine one, or more of the methods on the same work. I hope that the suggestion of ways of working will provide a start for the development of your own ideas.

Part 1 Raised or Relief Printing

Collage Blocks

The word *collage* is derived from the French verb *coller* which means 'to stick or glue'. A collaged block is a number of objects stuck down onto a base. This block may then be inked up in colour and printed.

For the base you need a firm material such as hardboard wood or strong card – about 12 × 8 ins (30 × 20 cm) is a good size to start with.

The glue must be strong and of the all-purpose-use variety. It should also spread thickly and readily.

A variety of small, easily found objects can be used. These may be made of materials such as metal, wood, plastic, paper or card or even natural found objects such as leaves and sticks. The block shown below is made from corrugated cardboard. A print from it is shown opposite.

The collaged block can be printed on many types of papers. Simple brown wrapping paper will give a different result to blotting paper. Lining paper is very inexpensive and available at most wallpaper and general stores. Most smooth papers are suitable. Try out the same block on a range of different papers and compare the results.

Spread the glue all over the base so that it is covered. Use a proper glue spreader or a piece of stiff card for this. Then stick those objects that you have chosen for your collage on

to the glue, so that when the glue is dry, the objects and materials will be held fast. Try not to let one object overlap another, except for very thin objects such as leaves, as this will make parts of the block stick up too much and cause difficulties with the printing.

Let the glue dry absolutely as it is rather thick; it is probably best to leave it overnight. Then the block can be printed.

Roll out some oil based, printing ink onto a small sheet of glass, a sheet of metal such as zinc, or a plastic laminated table top or work surface. The oil based printing ink can be purchased from an artists' materials or handicraft shop. You will also need some turpentine or white spirit and some rag for cleaning up. Roll the ink out on the work surface until it is flat and not too sticky and the roller is evenly covered all round. Then pass the roller over the surface of your block. When the ink can be seen to coat the top surface of the block, it is ready for printing. The more ink that is rolled onto the block, the denser the printed picture.

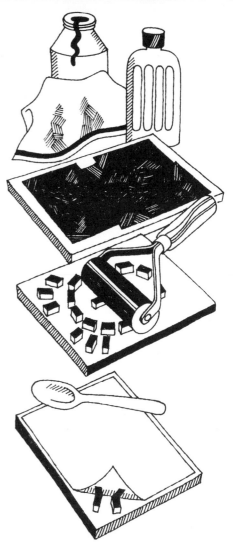

Hold the paper above the block then lower it gently onto the inked-up surface. When the paper comes in contact with the block the sticky ink will hold it lightly in place. Print by rubbing the back of the paper gently, with a dessert spoon, a wooden spoon, or your hand. If you hold the paper in place with one hand, you can lift up a corner with the other to see how it is printing. If it is too light it may need some more rubbing, or more pressure from the spoon or your hand. Otherwise it may need more ink, in which case, scrap that print and roll up the block again.

Here are some suggestions for ideas that you could do with collaged blocks. Collect together as many completely different small objects as you can find, such as pipe cleaners, hair pins, old wrappings, plastic doilies, dried peas, cup hooks, nuts, bolts, washers, springs, hair grips, paper clips, buttons, needles, buckles, milk bottle tops, old string vest, soap trays with sucker feet. You will then have a large number of objects to select from to make your collage.

You could make a design allowing the objects you choose to suggest ideas to you. For instance, a line of paper clips makes a very realistic fence. Make flowers out of blades, nuts and nails.

Try to depict a face solely from curtain rings of varying sizes.

Try making a landscape from dried peas and spaghetti with macaroni or pasta as trees and hedges. Use wire-wool and dried beans for sheep.

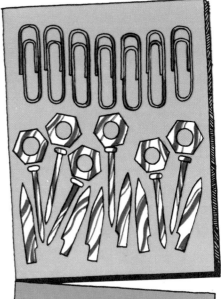

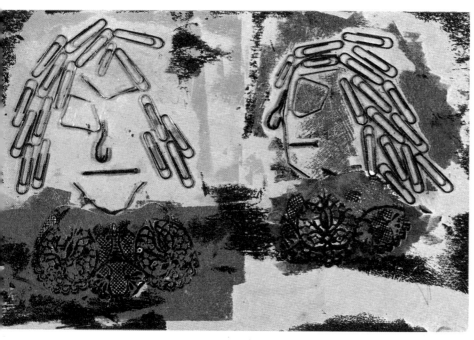

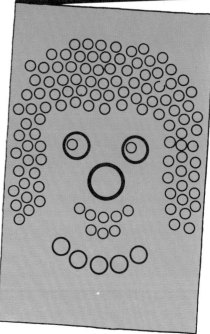

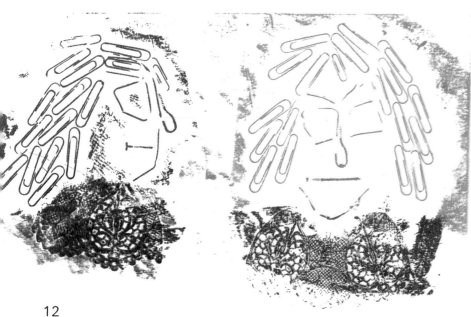

Why not make several separate blocks each depicting a different animal? Make one of the farmer – make his arms and legs out of toy knives and forks and his body a spoon; make his head out of paper clips and pipe cleaners or sewing needles and pins; give him a cup hook for a nose and two press-studs for eyes. Then print all the blocks on one sheet and use the farm picture as a setting for a collection of farm animals. You could then print them all in different colours.

Using small rollers charged with different colours you can roll up various areas of the same block in different colours.

Make a house using sheets of perforated metal for the walls, pencils for the roof and pieces of cloth for curtains. Cloth prints excellently; look for different textures such as corduroy, net, crimplene, lace and so on. Use bent wire to make a sun in your pictures. Make a family of 'pin men' from matchsticks and spills.

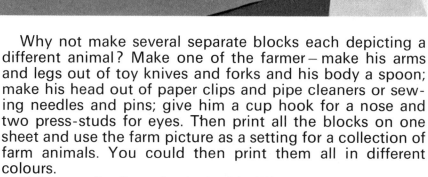

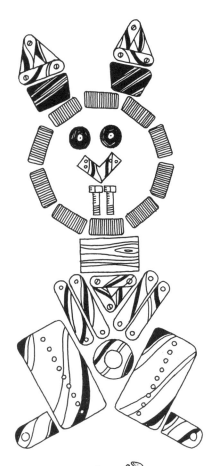

Think of your block not purely as a printing surface but as a piece of sculpture, a work of art in itself. When you have finished using it as a printing surface, if it is made of metal, it can be cleaned and polished, or you can paint it in bright colours. Then hang your block on the wall or use it in a toy theatre for one of the scenes, or put it in a dolls' house as a mural.

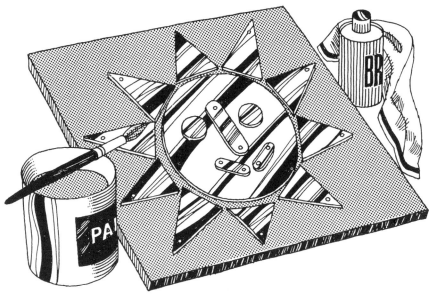

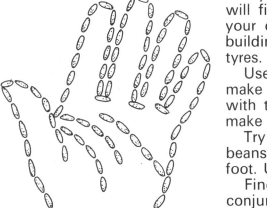

If you look at some of your discarded or broken toys you will find many bits and pieces that you can use well in your collaged blocks; flat plastic figures, springs, bits of building kits, old hinges, broken pen nibs, nails, wheels and tyres.

Use metal flanges, pieces of metal toys, flat brackets to make designs of subjects that have no direct connection with them. For example, use these mechanical objects to make a vase of flowers or an animal such as a rabbit.

Try making a block using the same type of object – all beans for instance, in a bean print of a face or a hand or foot. Use bent wire to form a face.

Find many different kinds of buttons and use these in conjunction with bits of card to make a block of a train with carriages. Make one carriage on a single block and print it many times in different colours on a long sheet of paper, to make a line of carriages.

Stick down different materials cut into squares, print them and then write on each one what kind of material it is so that you have a chart of printed materials.

For other ideas for pictures make a group of people, a file of soldiers, a traffic jam, a prize fight.

Why not print all your blocks on one large sheet as a catalogue of ideas?

String Prints

A *string print* is similar to a collaged block print in its construction, but instead of the vast range of differing materials suitable for collage, you use only string, but there are many varieties. String makes a print like a drawn line, but each sort of string has a different quality which gives the line a character. Line suggests rhythm and movement.

You must have a base of hardboard or thick card or some other material that does not warp. One 12 × 8 in (30 × 20 cm), or even smaller, is easily managed.

The glue should spread thickly and easily but does not need to be strong enough to stick metal.

Oiled string is not recommended as it resists most adhesives, but other than that, most types of string, tough yarn, or elastic bands, are suitable. Start collecting for a string box where you assemble a great variety of different strings and threads, then you will have a wide choice for your picture making.

Most smooth papers accept this kind of block readily and make attractive prints. Wrapping paper is the most available but special papers such as Japanese papers, which are very soft, but rather costly, lend themselves to this sort of print superbly. However, before spending money on high quality materials, try your blocks out on inexpensive lining paper, or *proofing*, paper to help you visualise how it is going to look in its final form.

Work out some idea of the picture beforehand, perhaps even making a small drawing for guidance. The reason for this is that long pieces of string are difficult to work with. It is easier if you have some idea before starting of what your string is drawing.

Thinly cover the base with glue and put the string directly onto this. Draw the picture with the string, cutting each length as you go. You might wish to draw it all with one piece of string, in which case, roll the string into a neat coil first and then just keep on unravelling the string and sticking it down without cutting it, until the work is finished.

When the drawing is complete it can be pressed down to help it stick, by placing a piece of card or hardboard on the top while it dries. If a piece of string becomes loose just stick this back individually. If the finished work does not look quite right you can pull off the string before it has completely dried, and re-glue it.

When the block is dry it is ready to print. Roll out some ink, in the way described in the previous chapter, and then roll up the surface of the string. Do it lightly at first until you are expert. You may be surprised to see, when the ink is on the string block, that it tends to only take on the top surface of the string and therefore your lines may be much thinner than you expected. If you want these lines to be heavier use a lot more ink and press quite hard with your roller.

Hold the paper above the block then lower it gently onto the inked-up surface. Hold it in place by putting a small weight on top of the paper or by holding it with your hand. Print by rubbing the back of the paper gently with a dessert spoon or a wooden spoon. A *bone folder* can also be used. These are used in bookbinding. The more ink that is rolled onto the block, the denser the printed picture.

If the string stuck down is roughly the same height all over the rubbing can be much harder and it is very often possible, especially when you use a wooden spoon, to rub, or *burnish*, the paper and see the impression showing through the back of the sheet.

It is also possible to take an excellent print from one of the string blocks without any ink, by placing a sheet of paper on the un-inked block, holding it still, and rubbing with a soft pencil or waxed crayon as you do when making a brass rubbing (see page 71).

Collecting pieces of string of various widths and lengths, see how many different types of string you can find – fine taut pieces, coarse fibrous pieces, parcel string, nylon or wire string, hairy or fluffy string, garden raffia, angora, double-knitting or 3-ply wool.

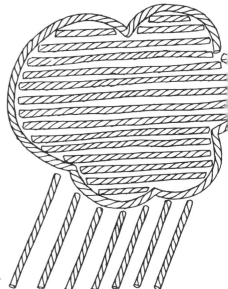

Make a design by allowing the quality of the string or thread to give you various ideas. Use the 'flowing' quality of a long piece of thin string, or the bristly ends of coarse string.

Start with simple shapes, try copying the outline of a toy train, or a teddy bear, or your mother. Make patterns, like cats' cradles, loose knitting, crocheting or knotting and secure them to a *knitting block*. Try criss-crossing long pieces to show waves breaking on the shore. Make a fish with the coarse parcel string, packed together in an oval shape.

Vary the type of string used on the same block to give a contrast of line and theme. Cut lots of short stubby pieces and fix onto the base in rhythmical lines to look like a cornfield blowing in the wind. Try cutting slightly longer pieces, clump them together and stick them onto the base on a background of corrugated card to make a field with stacks of hay already harvested. Glue different backgrounds to the base board, to stick your string onto.

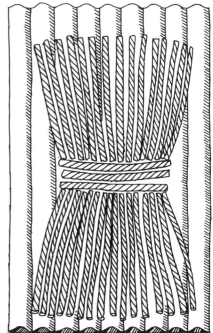

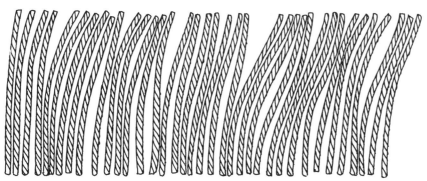

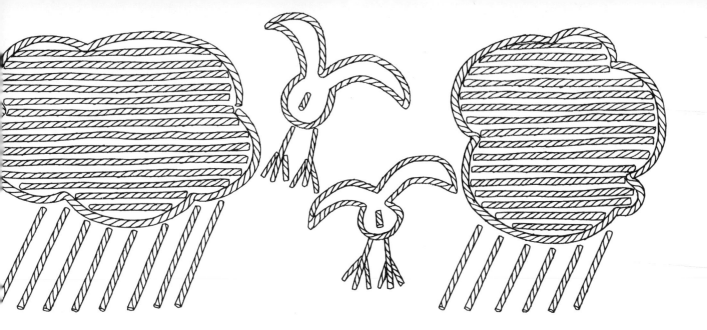

Use a large piece of card for a background and start by sticking string down in the shape of a bird, add a second bird or some clouds, put some horizontal lines inside some of the clouds to fill up the shape like dark rain clouds, put long thin diagonal strips for rain.

Create various faces. Cut short thick pieces for a 'crew cut' hairstyle and use a long thin piece to outline and draw the face, then use long pieces stuck closely together for long hair. Develop this idea and use very thick pieces for plaits, or make your own plaits out of thin string, which are then stuck down. Make some of these faces front face and some profile. Make some look old by using extra pieces of string for wrinkles on the forehead or 'crow's-foot' lines around the eyes. Make some look young, with wide big eyes and freckles, by coiling your string.

Try to make a face using only one piece of string without cutting it at all until you have finished. Then try making a line of simple figures from one long piece of string. They could be little dancing men, animals, monsters, or fishes swimming through the waves.

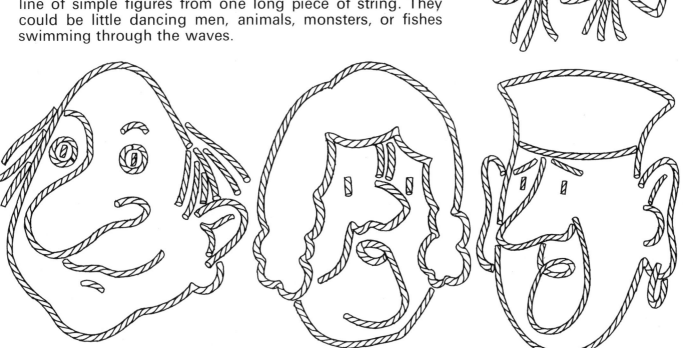

Why not design a clown, depicting his big baggy trousers out of folds of string and the pom-pom on his hat from a knot? Ink up your print heavily and thoroughly including large areas of backgrounds so that your drawing is surrounded by a white *halo*.

Make little blocks to produce your own Christmas cards. The *halo* method is particularly effective for pictures of angels, churches, or Christmas trees. They will seem to glow. If you can buy some metallic colours or use coloured paper, this could be exciting.

Alternatively, do not ink your block at all, but print only the top surface of the string by passing or rolling an inked roller over the back of the paper sheet placed on the block. This gives a very soft and delicate look to the print.

Use some of the smaller designs to paper the walls of a doll's house. Use a small block for wallpaper by repeating it many times on a large sheet of paper.

Try merging your inking colours on the roller, this is known as *rainbow printing*. It is particularly effective if you have made a block of a rainbow. You do this by putting out two colours, say red and yellow, on your inking slab. With the roller merge these colours so that you have orange in the centre, and then roll up the block. This is something that can be used in most printing methods.

If you make blocks of single animals then you could print them together on a large sheet of paper. Use string to show the bars of the cages. You could start to make a zoo.

Write your name in string, backwards, and use the block to 'sign' things with, as though it was a rubber stamp.

New York
ROME
London

Glue Prints

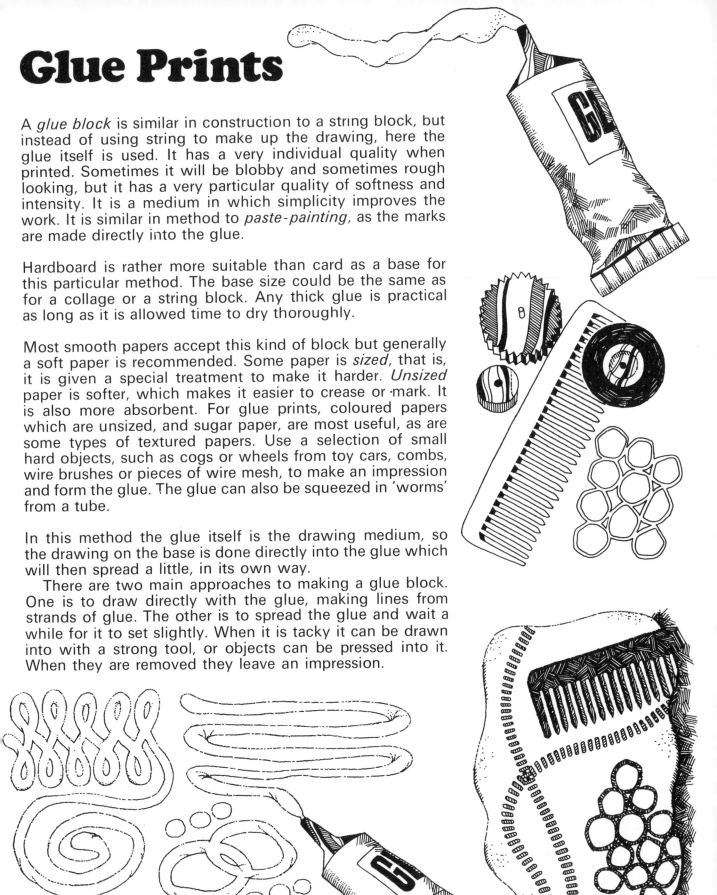

A *glue block* is similar in construction to a string block, but instead of using string to make up the drawing, here the glue itself is used. It has a very individual quality when printed. Sometimes it will be blobby and sometimes rough looking, but it has a very particular quality of softness and intensity. It is a medium in which simplicity improves the work. It is similar in method to *paste-painting*, as the marks are made directly into the glue.

Hardboard is rather more suitable than card as a base for this particular method. The base size could be the same as for a collage or a string block. Any thick glue is practical as long as it is allowed time to dry thoroughly.

Most smooth papers accept this kind of block but generally a soft paper is recommended. Some paper is *sized*, that is, it is given a special treatment to make it harder. *Unsized* paper is softer, which makes it easier to crease or ·mark. It is also more absorbent. For glue prints, coloured papers which are unsized, and sugar paper, are most useful, as are some types of textured papers. Use a selection of small hard objects, such as cogs or wheels from toy cars, combs, wire brushes or pieces of wire mesh, to make an impression and form the glue. The glue can also be squeezed in 'worms' from a tube.

In this method the glue itself is the drawing medium, so the drawing on the base is done directly into the glue which will then spread a little, in its own way.

There are two main approaches to making a glue block. One is to draw directly with the glue, making lines from strands of glue. The other is to spread the glue and wait a while for it to set slightly. When it is tacky it can be drawn into with a strong tool, or objects can be pressed into it. When they are removed they leave an impression.

Ink up the surface of the block thoroughly. The harder the roller the more the top surface is inked, the softer the roller the more the ink will spread into the block.

Lay the paper on top of the inked block. Take the print by applying pressure on the top surface of the printing paper. Use a rubber roller or a wooden spoon. This type of block can usually stand quite hard rubbing or burnishing.

Here are some ways of using the glue print.

Find any object that will make a track or impression in the glue; a comb, railway line, child's perforated building bricks, fork, or cheese grater. Use these objects to draw and shape your glue block. Use a fork to draw pine trees in the snow. Use a comb to make a corn field.

Try just making swirling patterns and print these in various colours, placing the block in different directions on a large sheet of paper.

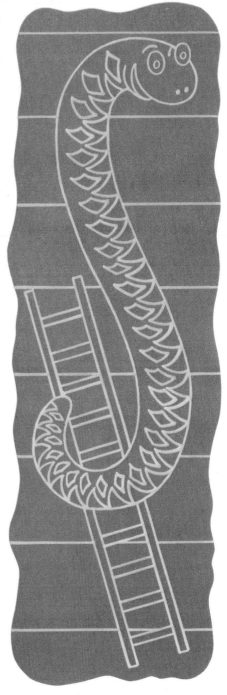

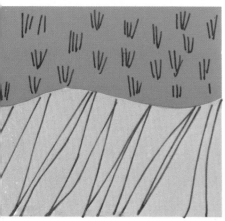

Design your own games like snakes and ladders or make your own maze. When the maze has been printed get other children to try to draw the correct route on it.

Here are some other ideas for glue pictures:
Try impressing screw-heads to represent crowds of people. Try different kinds of landscape from different countries, showing mountains, desert, trees. Draw strange animals with the glue. Use the glue in dots and try to make an outline portrait.

Make a seascape with boats, lighthouses, and rocks, or draw a cloud-scape with rooftops. Print your block in a dark colour and paint in coloured background areas.

Prints from Found Objects

A *found object print* is one that is made of assorted objects that are available and can be printed easily onto paper. The objects are not fixed to any base board but are inked up separately, and printed down onto paper directly. A complete print may be made from one large object, for example, a print can be taken from a fur glove without any addition to the print.

A variety of found objects of different types are needed for this sort of print, but they must print well. Some suitable objects to collect are rubber gloves, pieces of fur, the soles of shoes and even certain natural objects such as leaves and grasses, drift wood and shells. Any rubber object, such as a table mat, prints well.

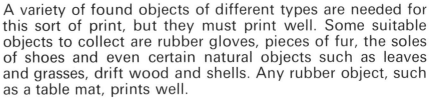

A soft thin paper is the most suitable for this type of printing. A Japanese paper is very useful and worth the extra expense as it prints in great detail. Lining paper is a good substitute.

Rollers are needed to roll up the found objects and an oil based ink should be used.

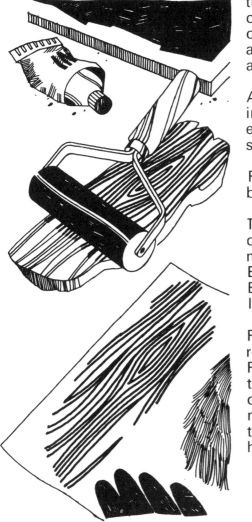

The best way to make a found object print is to print first one object then another onto a sheet of paper, or alternative material, in order to build up an idea by progressive stages. Each object becomes one element in the finished work. But in some cases, one single printed object, such as a large, interesting piece of wood, could be the whole print.

Roll up the first object by holding it still with one hand and rolling ink onto it with a fully charged roller held in the other. Position the object on the paper and press down carefully, to transfer the ink from the object to the paper. Lift up the object and look at the printed result before selecting the next object to be printed. Repeat the process. Each addition to the sheet will alter the existing work until a whole picture has been built up.

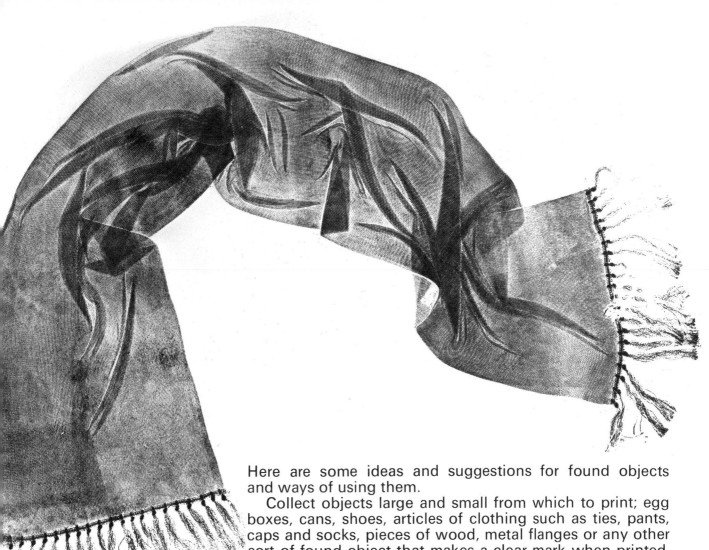

Here are some ideas and suggestions for found objects and ways of using them.

Collect objects large and small from which to print; egg boxes, cans, shoes, articles of clothing such as ties, pants, caps and socks, pieces of wood, metal flanges or any other sort of found object that makes a clear mark when printed.

Just print a selected object directly onto a piece of paper as it is, and then consider how the image has taken on a life of its own. Use the various objects to express an idea. Try two rubber gloves or string gloves shaking hands in friendship, or curled up as angry, striking fists.

Squash the egg box flat and use it as a printed texture. Flatten out a tin can, print the inside, the outside and both end surfaces, then cut out the print and try to reconstruct the three dimensional object.

Make soft delicate prints by using old net curtains, then use the textures for landscapes.

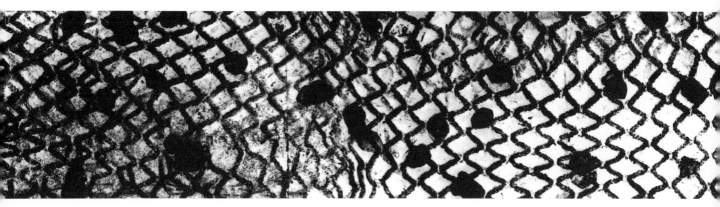

Print a self portrait using yourself as a found object. Put some lipstick on and kiss the paper for an impression of your lips. Use straw or string for your hair and the end of a pencil for freckles. Print your hands for the hands and your arms for the arms. Make the clothes up with texture taken from corrugated card or actual cloth. Use real buttons for buttons and string to outline the face. The print will be nearly life size and may soon take on a realistic and even recognisable look.

Try to make a forest or jungle by using thin metal to print a tree many times over, then add the leaves, animals, birds and creatures that live in the forest by making them up from your collection of found objects. Some really large prints can be made this way and you can combine your work with that of your friends if you discuss the ideas for the project with them first, and plan what you want to make.

Find as many different discarded gloves as possible. Print them down and compare the leather glove with the woollen glove and the lacy glove with the mitten.

Stamp Prints

A *stamp print* is closely related to a found object print in that certain types of found objects are printed by stamping. A typical example of a stamp print is the rubber stamp used in a post office to print the date on post office documents. These prints are made by stamping objects down onto an ink pad to charge them with colour, then pressing them down directly onto paper.

Collect some objects to be printed. They should receive ink readily and be small enough to hold in the hand. Your own hands make good stamp prints and so do fingers and feet. Old fashioned wooden type from a printers is always successful if it can be found. An old toy printing outfit is good too, especially if it has rubber pictures. Butter pats, or plastic numbers or letters from spelling sets can be used.

Ink or an inking pad can be bought at most stationers and they come in many colours, though the most usual are black and green.

Most kinds of paper are suitable for stamp prints, including newsprint and flimsy typing paper.

Work out the type of picture you want first. Choose your object and stamp it into the ink pad to charge it with ink, then onto the paper. If you stamp several times after one inking the image will get progressively lighter. Press it back into the ink pad when you want to make it bolder. Build up your design by adding more stamps.

The book jacket (above) was designed and printed by an eight-year-old boy using stamp prints.

Here are some pictures that you can make by stamp printing.

Create little animals and people using thumb and finger prints adding extra lines or paper clips for heads and tails.

Make your own book jackets by printing simple shapes of wood or rubber, or try to make your own record covers.

Cut out the shape of a bird in flight from a piece of rubber sheeting (it should be about $\frac{1}{4}$ in ($\frac{1}{2}$ cm) thick) and print it many times in various colours ranging from light to dark. Eventually you can build up a picture of a migration.

Use old wooden type to make posters. They could be used to advertise school activities. Use the letter forms to make words to label boxes. Use plastic numbers which are used on garden gates.

Print your own wallpaper on lining paper by using a motif such as a flower cut from rubber sheeting, printed down regularly.

Ask people with different sized feet to ink up the soles of their shoes and walk over a large piece of paper in different directions. Use pieces of old motor car tyres. Then compare the enormous differences that there are in the shapes and design.

Collect together a number of objects suitable for stamp printing, then invite some friends to work with you, taking turns to add to a group print. In this way you can develop a collective idea by discussing each stage as it takes on character.

Another approach to a group idea is to ink up a rubber ball and bounce it many times onto a large sheet of paper. The random marks may suggest ideas for further development so that you can add more consciously placed stamp marks. Ride a bicycle with inked-up tyres over a length of lining paper, or roll an inked-up hoop along it.

The immediacy of this method brings a sense of achievement. This will give self-confidence to those who feel worried about working in such a large printing area.

If you want to print more neatly and clearly, it is a good idea to use layers of newspaper as packing under the paper to be printed. This helps cushion the pressure and makes a sharply defined print.

See how many objects suitable for stamping can be bought for very small sums of money at the local department store. Decide on a certain figure. Set yourself a target of, say five items for that amount, and then come home and use them in a print.

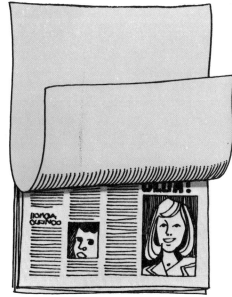

Lino Cuts

Lino cutting is the gouging or cutting away with cutting tools of the top surface of a piece of linoleum. The surface is then inked with a roller which leaves the cut or incised marks without ink. These cut away parts will be white, or, if you are printing on a coloured paper, they will be the colour of the paper.

For the lino block, a thick one-colour linoleum is best. It can be bought cheaply at most large household stores in off-cuts, or at artists' materials shops where it will be more expensive. The size will depend on your design. If, you use a piece of old lino, which may have some fascinating grain on it, it is easier to cut if it is heated slightly before use.

The strongest cutting tools are recommended. If you can afford it, a few well-chosen woodcarving tools are better than the *pen* type lino cutting tools which break easily.

It is easier if you draw on the block before cutting, with a marker pen or Indian ink.

The printing ink must be oil bound, so you will need white spirit or turpentine for cleaning up. It is also possible to buy a *reducing medium* to reduce the strength of the ink and make it transparent.

A soft paper is the best for this type of printing, and because the lino block is very strong, the paper should be quite tough. It must stand up to considerable rubbing or burnishing. For rough prints or *proofs*, lining paper is suitable.

Lino itself is easily cut to the required size and shape of the block as it can be scored with a sharp knife, then broken by hand. When your block is the right size, draw on your design with a marker pen or a brush and Indian ink.

When it is dry, cut away the areas which are to remain white. Always keep your hands behind the tool so that if it slips it will not cut you. Keep your cutting tools sharp for safety, as the more efficient the tool the less likelihood there is of accidents, as long as simple precautions are observed. *Always cut away from the body.* Keep on cutting until you want to take a print, then knock away spare shavings and bits of lino and roll up the block with black ink. Take a print or proof as you would when printing a string print. Clean off the ink with turpentine or white spirit and carry on cutting as soon as the block is dry. The block has to be held still with your left hand or with a *jig* (see glossary, p. 76).

Set up the ink as you would to print a string print. However, aim for a flatter, more even film of ink on the roller and the block. The final print may have a shiny surface. This may be because of varnish in the printing ink, the amount of ink used, or the *size* on the paper.

When the surface of the block is evenly and quite thickly charged with ink, the paper must be placed down carefully. The ink is then transferred to the paper either by rolling on the back with a clean roller, or by burnishing. This can be done with a wooden spoon, the handle of a cutting tool or your finger nail. The print must then be separated from the block very carefully to avoid damage to the paper. The block must then be cleaned and allowed to dry before re-inking.

Try cutting a piece of lino with as many types of cutting tools as possible, as they all make different marks and will ink up in a variety of ways.

There are two main approaches to the cutting of lino blocks. They may, of course, be used in combination with each other in the same block. In the *white line method* you cut your design directly into the lino leaving large areas of block to be inked up, bordered by white lines. The alternative is the *black line method* in which large non-printing areas are cut away leaving only the lines to print.

Using a fine cutting tool, try making several simple line blocks such as a man running for a bus, and then print them alongside each other in sequence, as a cartoon or story.

Make a block or a series of blocks to be printed in repitition on a fabric for cushion covers or a beach bag.

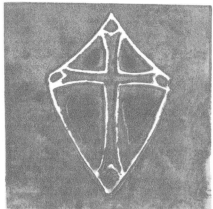

There is a very simple but effective way of producing a colour print using the same piece of lino. Cut the lino a little to show the basic lines of your design. Then take a number of prints from it in a colour, say yellow. Clean up the block, allow it to dry and then cut away more of the design. Print this on top of the previous printing and in the same position in a second colour, say red. This can be repeated to add more and more fine detail until no lino remains. The final colour may be black to accent certain areas of the design. This is known as the *elimination method*.

Try making lino pictures, using the elimination method, of everyday still-life objects such as a cup and saucer, a toy car or a chair. Cut a block to be printed in one colour to make party invitations. The lettering prints as a *mirror image* so it must be cut in reverse in order to be read the right way round.

After you have had some experience of lino cutting try cutting the edge of the lino block in the shape of the object you are depicting, such as an aeroplane or a car. Then print more than one on a sheet of paper. Print many different shaped blocks on one sheet of paper.

Lino is a suitable medium to print many surfaces with for a dolls' house or stage set. You could print onto fabric for carpets, curtains and soft furnishings. You could also make matching wallpaper. You could cover matchbox furniture that you have made. Make a poster to advertise your school play, film society, or jumble sale, or print admission tickets. It is possible to print literally thousands of copies from one tough lino block.

After some cutting experience you may choose to try cutting wood instead of lino. You will notice several differences.

If you use small rollers you can often apply several colours to different areas of one block, thereby getting a colour print with one printing.

Try cutting firectly into lino without a preliminary drawing and see if this gives a more interesting final print. Try cutting three blocks separately. Print them in order, one on top of the other in different colours. It is very easy to combine lettering with design in a lino block, so try writing a short book and cutting both the text (backwards) and illustrations together.

For someone who likes to work slowly and deliberately, lino cutting is an ideal medium.

Potato and Vegetable Prints

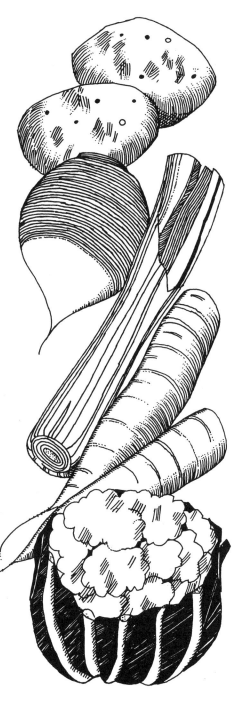

A *potato print* is one of the simpler forms of printing. It is a form of stamp print in which a potato or other similar vegetable is used to make the mark. The vegetable is cut in half and is then printed, either using the shape it has, or with marks gouged out of it.

Use any firm vegetable such as a potato, a swede or a parsnip. It should be reasonably large as the work has to be bold, not too detailed. You can also cut a cauliflower or firm cabbage or leek in half and print from this.

Inks should be *water based* as the potato contains a great amount of water. Ordinary powder paint applied with brushes can be used for this type of printing too.

Most papers are suitable as long as they are not shiny. A simple cartridge is probably the most suitable. Lining paper tends to crinkle too much, due to the amounts of water in both the potato and ink.

Cut a potato in half to make two flat surfaces. Let it dry for a few minutes. Then gouge or cut a simple design or shape in one of the two halves of the potato. Holding the potato in one hand, paint the flat surface that you have cut, with a brush dipped in water based paint or ink; then stamp it onto the paper, using the same method as for stamp prints.

This method is particularly useful when a simple and direct pattern is wanted. In a repeating pattern it will have an interesting irregularity because of the difficulty of placing the potato in exactly the right position each time.

Potatoes and other vegetables tend to shrivel up when used, so that they cannot be used for more than one session of printing.

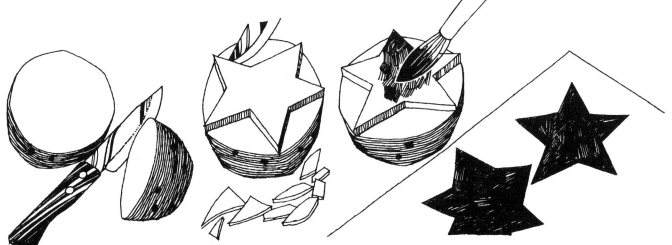

Although this is a very quick, simple and rather un-sophisticated method, some people have even decorated their walls with potato prints, using the potato to get the effect of clouds and of blossom on a tree.

Look for potatoes that are not round or have an unusual outside shape and try to use this shape in the design by cutting across this section. For example, use a curved potato to print a new moon, or an oblong or pear shape could be a wobbly man.

A selection of circular shapes will make various different faces for people sitting in a train or standing in a bus queue. To make the faces appear different in some cases, cut away the background, leaving sections for the eyes; nose and mouth which stand up, *in relief*. With other potato faces leave the shape of the potato and gouge holes for the features. Alternatively, change the outside shape, make a hair line or double chin, but leave enough potato in the centre to cut out the features.

Print your various faces on one large sheet of paper, stamping them down all over the sheet to represent a football crowd. Try printing them in various colours using the same block as often as you please. Print faces in curved rows, with smaller ones at the back, like people at the cinema, or a crowd watching a pop group.

Print a wall with some other printmaking method such as card prints, or take a rubbing from the wall itself, and print a line of potato faces looking over this wall.

Cut a simple shape of one bird or one animal, and print it dozens of times to show them in flocks or herds.

Draw, paint or print a tree. Cut a bird out of the potato and print it, so that there are dozens of birds perched on a tree. Print them in various colours.

Try cutting the shape of simple traffic signs and write what each one stands for. Print the correct colours; for example, a red and white warning triangle, or print red, orange and green circles for traffic lights. Design and print your own traffic signs. If you have a model village or car circuit you could print on card and use a matchstick base to stand them by the roadside. Make a big mural by sticking some large sheets together and print all the signs on it.

If you have a toy theatre, try printing the 'flats' and back-cloth.

Try making simple pictures of objects or plants that would be easy to print with a potato, such as a daffodil with a trumpet, a daisy with petals, or a dish of apples. When printing the apples, paint on the potato the colours from green to red.

Print on to small pieces of card and use these for gift tags.

Cut out some basic shapes, a square, a circle, and a triangle and print an all-over pattern with a repeating sequence. Decorate the side of boxes either directly onto the box or onto sheets of paper, which is then cut out and stuck onto boxes.

Print various shapes on both sides of a sheet of card, then cut the card out into oblongs or bell shapes or circular shapes and make Christmas decorations.

Try printing in thick, white and light bright colours onto black paper. Think of various ideas that can be printed onto a black background. Print a vase of flowers. The petals can all be printed with the same potato and the variations will be shown in the irregularities of the technique.

Try printing as many different shapes of potato as possible onto a sheet of printing paper in various colours. Cut these out and stick them onto another sheet of paper to make a new design, thus making a paper *collage*.

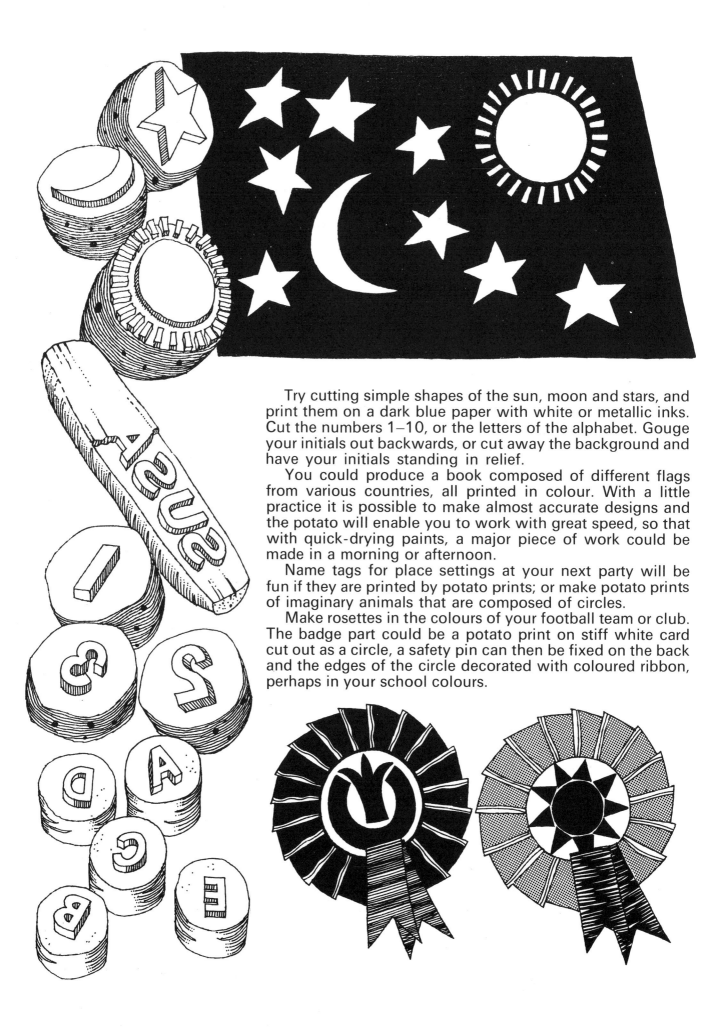

Try cutting simple shapes of the sun, moon and stars, and print them on a dark blue paper with white or metallic inks. Cut the numbers 1–10, or the letters of the alphabet. Gouge your initials out backwards, or cut away the background and have your initials standing in relief.

You could produce a book composed of different flags from various countries, all printed in colour. With a little practice it is possible to make almost accurate designs and the potato will enable you to work with great speed, so that with quick-drying paints, a major piece of work could be made in a morning or afternoon.

Name tags for place settings at your next party will be fun if they are printed by potato prints; or make potato prints of imaginary animals that are composed of circles.

Make rosettes in the colours of your football team or club. The badge part could be a potato print on stiff white card cut out as a circle, a safety pin can then be fixed on the back and the edges of the circle decorated with coloured ribbon, perhaps in your school colours.

Part 2 Flat Surface Printing

Transfer Drawing and Monoprinting

Transfer drawing is a method of transferring ink from a flat surface onto a sheet of paper with pressure. A *monoprint* is made by painting onto a surface and blotting it with the printing paper. Both of these two methods have a very individual look. Monoprinting has an organic and natural quality and transfer drawing has a distinctive soft line.

The base that you are printing from should be similar to any inking-up slab such as a sheet of glass or plastic laminate. Ink can be oil paint or oil-bound printing ink. In some ways, oil paint is better for making monoprints.

Paper should be thin and porous enough to take the ink. A rubber roller and some paint brushes are needed. The paint brushes should be of the bristle kind that are used for oil painting.

Monoprinting is even simpler and consists of painting in fairly diluted oil-bound inks onto a base slab and carefully placing a sheet of paper on top. Pressure is placed on the back of the sheet of paper, usually by hand, sometimes with a roller, and this will pick up the ink from the block. Those who enjoy the freedom of painting will find this a most attractive method of printing.

A useful way of developing the monoprint is to use a slab of glass for the base and to put a line drawing of the subject underneath the glass. If the printing paper is then pinned down on one side with drawing pins, it is possible to pull back the paper, clean the glass with white spirit and then paint again onto the glass, still using the line drawing. In this way one can add to the print accurately, using the drawing as a key. Roll the printing paper back across the glass, making sure it does not slip out of *register*.

To make a transfer drawing, roll out a very thin film of printing ink onto a printing slab. It should be smooth, tacky, dust free and not at all wet. Gently lower the printing paper onto the slab so that it is resting so lightly that the paper is hardly picking up any ink. The print is made by drawing on to the back of the sheet of paper with any hard tool or instrument, such as the pointed end of a paint brush or a ballpoint pen. Using a pen or biro is useful as you can see what you are drawing. However it is not necessary. This method is very quick and has a surprising autographic quality of line when it is lifted off the slab, and the print is seen. Hand pressure can be used to create areas of *tonal contrast*; greys and blacks.

Start by making a transfer drawing and find out the distinctive types of line and marks obtained with this method. Vary the tool you draw with. This will change the character of the line. Use a soft pencil for a more blurry, wider line, and a pair of compasses for a thin sharp line. Try using a knitting needle or the handle of a brush. Rub with your fingers to make a background tone. Scribble consistently over one area to obtain a rich, dense area.

Make your paper larger than your slab so that you can get a white border round your work. Instead of using just black on the slab, use patches of colour so that your line drawing is in a variety of colours.

Transfer printing is a very good method for drawing your own cartoons. Try and make up your cartoon characters. Illustrate your own or someone else's poems and try to incorporate the poem with the drawings. Develop this idea to create your own book, either with simple black and white drawings or using several colours. Then bind the drawings together or use a plastic holder. Mount your drawings onto card and make a calendar with them. Or you could use them as greetings cards for birthdays or Christmas or for party invitations.

This is a very productive printing method so draw quickly, or even scribble, subjects such as a Christmas scene or an angel. The finished print takes only the same amount of time as it takes to complete the drawing.

Cut printed figures out and mount them on card leaving tabs on either side. Bend them round and glue them so they stand up. They can then be used as characters in a model theatre, soldiers in battle or knights in armour. Make miniature paintings to hang on the walls of your dolls' house, or a frieze design to decorate it with.

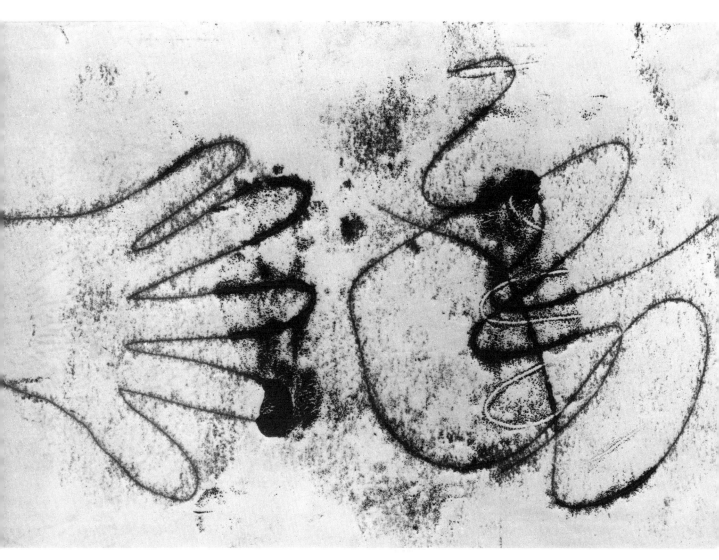

Although there is a large element of chance in this method, with experience it can be controlled to a considerable extent. By varying the consistency of the ink you can achieve different effects. It is possible to print a thick texture with something of the character of an oil painting. It is equally possible to produce a print which is light and delicate, both in texture and in colour.

Try making a portrait of someone you know well, using a stick to draw with so that you cannot see what you are drawing as you go along. Compare this with a second drawing of the same person done when looking at the sitter and at the paper, and consider which looks the most like the person.

Put a reproduction of your favourite painting under the glass base, as described earlier, and make your own interpretation of the painting, by painting on the glass. Take a print off the glass, then pin the print and the reproduction side by side and compare them.

Monoprinting and transfer drawing are very useful as an introduction to printmaking as a whole; experience can be gained quickly because of the immediacy of these methods and the cheapness of the materials and equipment.

Roller Offset

A *roller offset* print is an image that has been printed onto paper from a roller, usually one made of soft gelatine. The object is *offset* from its surface to the roller and then onto the paper. The first stage is to get an impression of the object onto the roller. A very precise image including considerable detail can be made this way. It is a useful technique for printing objects which do not normally lend themselves to printing, such as scissors or a pair of spectacles.

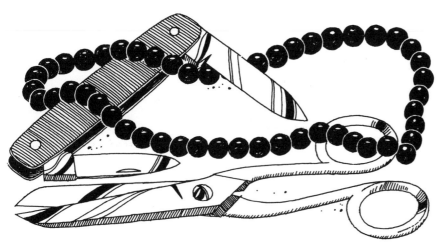

You will need a selection of objects to make the print with. These can be three dimensional such as a necklace, a pen-knife or various tools. One soft gelatine roller is necessary and this should be as large as you can afford. The ink has to be an oil based printing ink and can be of any colour. A rubber roller and an inking-up slab are also needed. This can be of glass or plastic laminate.

Any smooth surfaced paper will do for this particular method, even a shiny paper. An *art* paper or card will pick up the most detail.

Roll out the usual square of ink with a rubber or gelatine roller, then with this roller, ink up the object to be printed. Take another perfectly clean soft gelatine roller, and while holding the object in one hand, pass the soft roller over the inked object. The image of it will now be seen clearly on the roller and can be printed down onto a sheet of paper.

The way to do this is to press the roller slowly and firmly down in position on the paper, and roll the roller slowly over the printing paper. With a little practice it is possible to position the image exactly where it is needed on the printing paper. The gelatine roller must be cleaned between each offsetting, and allowed to dry.

Don't make the mistake of rolling the roller round more than once for each offsetting, or you will get a double image. You may be surprised at how much of a surface you can cover with one turn of a fairly large roller

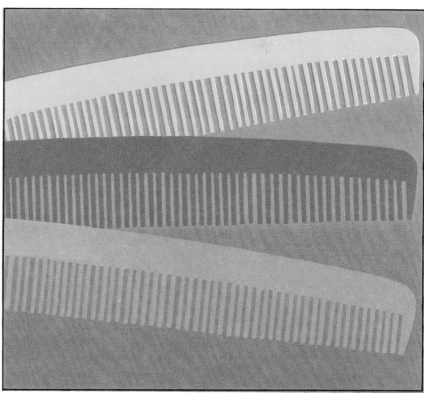

First gather together a variety of flattish objects which have a surface capable of holding ink. Choose as many of the most unusual or unlikely objects you can find: the lettering indented on the side of a glass bottle, a flat lead soldier, or the side of a small metal toy car, or wire mesh.

Try to print all of these by the roller offset method and see how they come out. Then decide which ideas you would like to develop.

Print the roller more than once without cleaning it and inking it up again, see how the fainter image compares with the heavier one. Print the same object many times in different colours on a sheet of paper. Try printing a large object or the brickwork on the wall of a building that is too large and immovable to be printed in any way except with an offset roller.

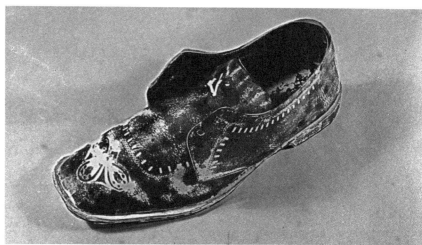

Try taking prints from all the different parts of a shoe. Cut them out and try to reconstruct the shoe itself. Do the same with a telephone or a basket of leaves, or a hat.

If you know of a room where you can take prints off the actual doors and walls, you will be able to make large prints and even reconstruct the whole room from them. You might be allowed to do this in an old shed, a kitchen where the walls can be washed down afterwards, or a room that is just about to be redecorated – but always ask permission first. Start by making an offset print of a keyhole, then a key to go with it. Let the idea grow from these to the handle, then the door itself. There might be a light switch, coathooks, panelling, skirting board, and textured wallpaper before the picture is finished. This is a good way of making up stage *flats* for a play.

Roll up a set of kitchen utensils and print them in a line, as though they were hanging on a wall. Do the same thing with tools from a toolbox. Stick them onto a cardboard box to make a replica toolkit. Take an offset print of a knife, fork and spoon and make a print of a table set for a meal. Try printing this onto plastic sheets and make them into table mats. Use other printing methods you have tried to solve the problem of representing the food.

You could use these prints to decorate an attractive folder, for recipe cuttings, or for all those instruction leaflets that come with tools and gadgets.

Stencils

A *stencil print* is made by using a sheet of stencil paper with cut out shapes that mask out areas of the printing paper. When ink is forced through or rolled on top of the printing paper, the stencil prevents the negative areas receiving the ink. The stencil is then lifted up and the shapes show up clear and positive. Stamped wax paper stencils of the alphabet or of simple pictures can be bought in stationers' shops, but there are many simple ways of making stencils yourself.

For the *mask* or stencil use waxed paper, stencil paper or thin card. Ordinary paper can be used but it will tend to tear during printing. For cutting you need scissors and a sharp knife. The inks can be of many types. It is possible to use water based printing inks, coloured writing inks, oil based printing inks, felt tipped and marking pens.

For printing, use sponges, stencil brushes from your local art shop, paint brushes or rollers.

Any type of paper can be used to print on, but stencils can be applied to fabrics, to wall surfaces, furniture and many kinds of three dimensional objects, such as building blocks. The stencil method can be used for many decorative purposes as well as picture making.

Make your first stencil by cutting holes into a very thin sheet of card. What you cut away will print. You can make a drawing for your design and then trace it onto the stencil paper. You then cut the stencil. After you have printed it you can cut more of the stencil away and then match the stencil up with the first printing, and print again. This gives you a second colour, and the colour which is made where it overprints the first gives a third colour.

Alternatively, you can print your first stencil on several sheets of paper. When it is dry, you can use one of the prints as the stencil for the second printing. If you leave the areas already printed and cut some other part away, your print will have two separate colours. You can build up in this way to make a print with several colours on it.

Stencil using sponge

One stencil printing method is to lay your stencil on top of your printing paper and hold it in place with some weights – kitchen weights are ideal. Then spray, using a fixative spray and some water based ink (see page 57). When the mask or stencil is lifted, the design is left.

Having made the stencil you can apply the ink in many different ways. It is possible to paint the stencil design or dab the colour on with a sponge. If a flat, evenly inked stencil is required, use a gelatine roller charged with ink and press it down, rolling across the stencil. The stencil must be thin to enable a sharp edge to be printed. Tape the stencil onto the paper to prevent it from sticking to the roller and tearing.

It is possible, if the stencil has several separate cut out shapes, to print these in various colours by using a number of rollers each charged with a different colour.

A stencil brush loaded with paint can be dabbed onto the stencil to create a *stippled* effect.

Stippled stencil

Stencil using roller

Stencilling is one of the most practical means of printing onto fabric. It is a simple procedure but works very well. The sharpness of the edge can provide a contrast with the texture of the material itself, and the effect of stippling or dabbing with a sponge will give a very varied half tone grading from light to dark, and an opportunity to develop a variety of textures.

Commercial stencils of letters and numbers and even cut outs of fruits, signs, symbols and other assorted objects, are available inexpensively at stationers and art shops. Drawing aids in chemistry outfits made of thin plastic will also do. These can be used as the basis for imaginative ideas.

Try using the same stencil in many ways and with many different methods of printing. Use felt-tipped pens, ballpoint pens, inked rollers and paint dipped sponges.

Using stencil paper or thin card, cut out some of your own stencils. One easy way of doing this is to draw round an object and cut the shape out. Try printing the cut out object as a stencil, and then the sheet it was cut from, thereby printing the same shape as a positive and a negative as well.

Ask someone to try and copy your shadow on a wall. Use your own hand and foot as a stencil. Try drawing simple silhouettes of animals and flowers. Draw a single figure dancing with arms and hands spread out. Print several of them in a line, cut the print out and hang it as a Christmas decoration.

Look around the house for objects, or a saw from the tool box. Draw round them, cut them out and build up a design using them several times. Try using both the positive and the negative of these.

Use ready made lettering stencils to make brightly coloured labels for school books, storage jars and boxes.

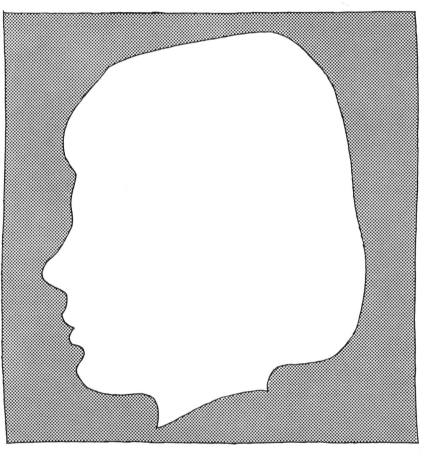

Cut out stencils of the large land masses of the world, then use stencil letters to mark the names of the different countries.

Make designs with a tool by punching holes in paper, without tearing or cutting. Try to make a design by using the edge of a sheet of paper moving it as you print. Use different types of edges, such as a torn edge, or a burnt edge of paper (make sure an adult is in the room when you do this). Try a jagged edge, cut with fabric pinking shears. Make a number of different stencils to be printed in different colours in the same print.

Discover other different ready made objects that can be used easily as stencils, such as plastic doilies, perforated flower pot holders, cheese graters of different sorts. Print these by *splattering*, using a scrubbing brush, tooth or nail brush, or use a stencil brush to stamp the colours into the holes.

It is possible to create a textured surface by placing sand-paper or rough cloth, or embossed wallpaper, under the printing paper.

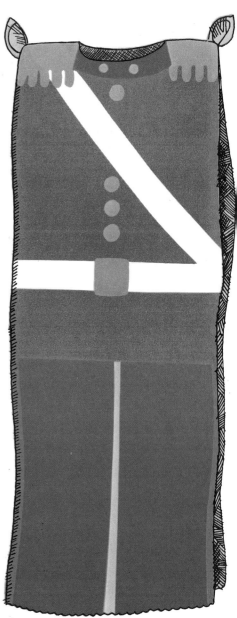

Use stencils to print on chairs, decorative walls in your own room, and decorate cardboard boxes, or a table top. Use stencils to paint the 'flats' in your school play. Print illustrations of toys and games on the doors of a toy cupboard. Try stencilling onto acetate and use it for lampshades.

Print onto fabric and make simple clothes such as a tie or scarf. Use stencils to add detail to costumes for a play or fancy dress. Print these onto a ready made paper bag.

Print bird shapes, or faces, and cut them out. Hang them on wires to make a mobile that moves in the wind. Stencil angels with large wings for a Christmas mobile. While the ink is still wet, dust them with glitter.

A series of small stencils can be used to make your own book. In a story, the trees in the background and some of the characters can appear many times.

Try printing a figure on a piece of material, then sew it up for use as a glove puppet or stuff it as a soft toy, which would make a pleasing present for someone.

Spray Prints

A *spray print* is any print produced with a spray. It is similar to a stencil print in that a *mask* is needed. Instead of a flat stencil, any object may be positioned on the paper or fabric, and sprayed. When it is lifted off, the shape is seen in negative form. When a cut stencil is used and then sprayed, the shape is a positive.

For a simple and efficient spray which is easy to clean, the best type is probably a fixative spray. They are sold cheaply in any art shop. Aerosol cans of spray paint can be used, but great care must be taken to prevent the paint getting everywhere. Never let spray get near anyone's eyes, nose or mouth.

Inks can be water based and must be liquid in consistency. This does not apply to spray paint, as white spirit is usually needed for cleaning up. *Gouache* or *powder paint* are quite adequate for most prints. A container to mix the paint in about the size of a tumbler or small coffee tin is also needed; also a pair of scissors or a knife to cut stencils.

You should collect a variety of objects that have a distinctive shape either in profile, such as keys or forks, or that have holes in them that the spray will get through, such as paper clips, lace curtains or paper doilies.

Most papers and materials can be sprayed on. White cartridge is ideal for this purpose. The only paper that is not suitable is the shiny variety.

Place a variety of small objects on a sheet of printing paper. Pour some coloured ink into a container and put one end of the spray in the mixture. Blow gently through the other end and a spray will be thrown out which will cover the objects and the paper. Remove the object, and there is the print! The distance that the ink is blown from makes for textural characteristics, and this can be varied considerably. Blowing harder makes a difference too.

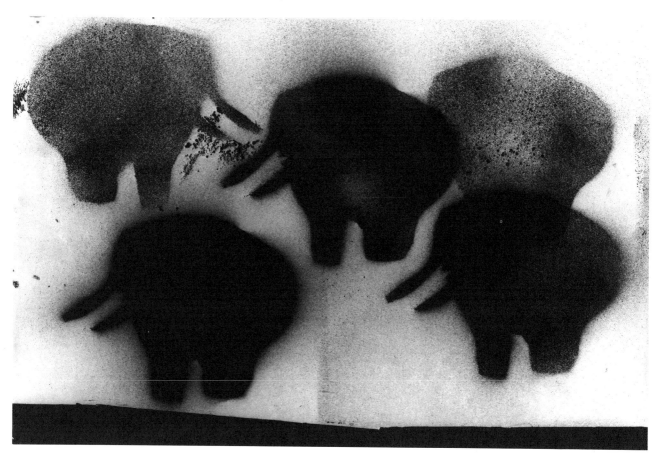

Lay a lace curtain which is no longer wanted on a sheet of printing paper. Spray various colours onto it from different containers. The resulting print will be very delicate, and full of subtle variations.

Try spraying a knife, fork and a spoon, then move them and spray again. See how the varying density affects the print.

Spraying a three dimensional object from all sides so as to describe the three dimensions in the print. Use a water based ink to spray round your hand. Combine spray prints with stencils. Spray the background of your paper before you start the print.

If you have a model theatre, try spraying on acetate to create special effects such as a snow storm.

Try cutting a paper stencil of flowers. Apply it to an old shirt holding it in place with clips and spray it with a fabric dye. Use lettering to put a slogan or image on a T shirt. Moving the stencil slightly and spraying again will give a different look to the work.

Use simple stencils and spray onto curtains to make them more decorative and colourful.

Transfer Rubbing

A *transfer rubbing* is a print which incorporates photographs in black and white or in colour, taken from magazines. These are transferred from the magazine to the print by rubbing. Several different images can be put onto the same sheet of paper in this way. Lettering, photographs, or already-printed drawings or a combination of these can be built up in the same way that a collage or 'sticking' is made.

Sort out and cut from magazines and comics as many photographs, advertisements and drawings as you like. Choose some that have a strange or personal feel to them. Collect any printed image from these sources if you think it may be of use to you in making your print. You have to remember that when they are transferred, they will show in reverse, so that words will not be readable.

White spirit or turpentine is needed as a solvent to help the transferring process. A soft pencil, or bone folder, as used in bookbinding, is used to rub the pictures onto the paper.

The paper should be flat and smooth but not too flimsy. Cartridge paper is ideal for this purpose.

Take one of the photographs to be transferred, put it face down, and with a brush or other implement, coat the back of the photograph with white spirit or turpentine so that it soaks for about three minutes. This loosens the ink on the printed surface. Then place this prepared image face down on the printing paper. Hold it down firmly with one hand and with the other, rub or burnish every bit of the back of the photograph with the bone folder or the soft pencil.

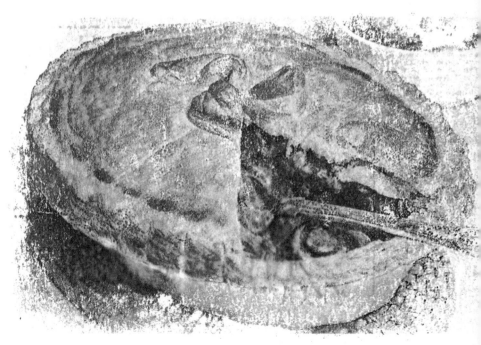

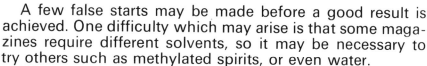

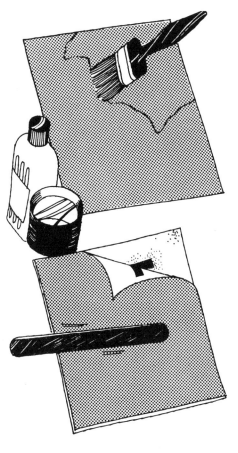

A few false starts may be made before a good result is achieved. One difficulty which may arise is that some magazines require different solvents, so it may be necessary to try others such as methylated spirits, or even water.

When one image has been printed in this way, try adding to it with other pictures or photographs to build up a complete picture. During the process of rubbing, try lifting up a corner of the photograph to check if it is transferring well. If it is too light it can be rubbed over again until it shows up more strongly.

Two copies of the same magazine will give you the possibility of duplicating the same photographic material. This will allow you to use the identical image twice on the same sheet of printing paper.

Other printing methods can be used in conjunction with a transfer rubbing. Try using a spray stencil or a stamp print in combination with this method.

The larger your basic collection of coloured and black and white printed material suitable for this purpose, the better. This enables you to be really selective when forming the idea for your print. Try experimenting with labels from packets and jars, such as jam-jar labels.

Collect cards from tea or cereal packets, images printed on paper bags, used postage stamps and cheese labels, or paper which is used to wrap fruit. Seek out pictures that seem to go together, or that look humorous together. You could make up some very amusing advertisements for imaginary products.

Try making a joke book, with pages cut so that it is possible to fold the book showing a head, a body, and legs that are interchangeable with those on other pages. You could include a monkey too.

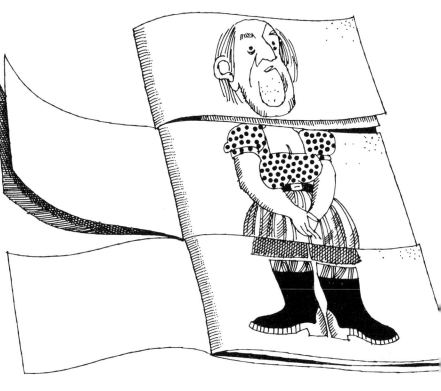

Make an enormous landscape, or a jungle mural over a long period of time. Add bits to the print as you come across suitable trees, people, animals, clouds, sun, plants and grasses. Keep on building it up until every part of the print is covered.

Transfer diagrams or drawings of machinery. These may suggest a new starting point to work from.

Make up strange images by putting unlikely objects together disregarding size and perspective. Use black and white photographs and coloured ones in combination.

Find examples of all the different styles of lettering you can and put as many down on a sheet of paper as possible.

Choose a subject that interests you, such as the history of costume, then print a sheet of dresses of the same period. Do this for motor cars, aeroplanes or trains. Try to make a simple book. You could make a zig-zag number book with the printed numbers from 1 to 10. Make a miniature newspaper or magazine. Transfer print some cartoons, then change them a little or add to them so they become your own idea.

Transfer rubbing is a useful technique to provide illustration for a project of local interest. Find a large black and white photograph of a town and put in brightly coloured murals and hoardings to make the town look more exciting. Do a similar project by redesigning your own town and carry this out by drawing the idea, and adding rubbings to those parts of the drawing that need photographic imagery.

Make a mural using photographs of all your favourite film stars or pop singers and have it hanging on your wall.

Use images in advertisements to make your own advertisements and ideas for posters.

Card Prints

Card prints are made from pieces of card that have been cut into varying shapes, rolled up in ink and printed. It is a very inexpensive and direct method of printing. It enables flat colours to be printed freely and blocks to be made quickly.

Sheets of thin card are probably the easiest to start with as they can be cut easily with a pair of scissors or a sharp knife. Most types of card can be used. A textured card will print the texture, so if a flat colour is required, smooth card must be used, but it might be a good idea to try using thick textured or embossed wallpaper. You will also need cutting tools such as knives or scissors, and oil based printing inks, a rolling-out slab of glass or plastic laminate for the ink, and rubber or gelatine rollers for inking up the card.

Some kind of improvised press is useful for card printing. A metal pinch press, or even just a piece of plank wood to put on top of the printing paper to increase the pressure will do. Failing a press, a wooden spoon can be used to rub or burnish.

Most types of smooth absorbent papers are suitable for this method of printing.

Draw an image or design on a sheet of card 12 × 8 ins (30 × 20 cms). Simplify the drawing and eliminate unnecessary detail, reducing it to straightforward shapes. This is because the different shapes have to be cut out separately. Anything very small will cause problems when you come to ink up and print and will not necessarily improve the design.

Having cut out the card into the various pieces, ink them up separately with the different colours you have chosen. Fit them back together as you would in a jigsaw, so you re-assemble the complete design inked up in colour.

Lay a sheet of printing paper on top, and over this, carefully place a plank of wood or a strong box laid on its side. If this is done on the floor of the studio, art room or play room, you can stand on the plank to exert pressure. This transfers the ink from the card to the printing paper. The amount of pressure will depend on your weight.

If there is no press and the plank method is not practical, then you must burnish the back of the paper. Keep checking on how the print is progressing by lifting up a corner of the printing paper to see what is happening, and how evenly the work is printing. Take care not to move the pieces of inked up card as you burnish.

Pieces of card printed this way will show white lines round the edge of each shape. Often this is not important, but just a characteristic of this type of print. If it spoils the design, then it is possible to print each piece of the jigsaw separately. Matching up the second piece of card along the exact edge of the first printed colour, and the white lines will be eliminated.

Sometimes it may be necessary to roll up a piece of card a second time and reprint it on top of the first printing to get enough ink on it for a smooth texture. Roll up with plenty of ink, as card is absorbent.

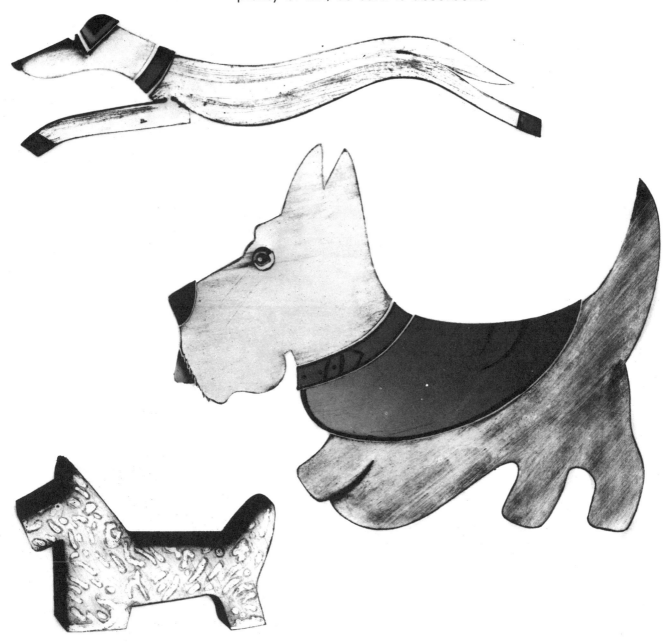

Mangle press

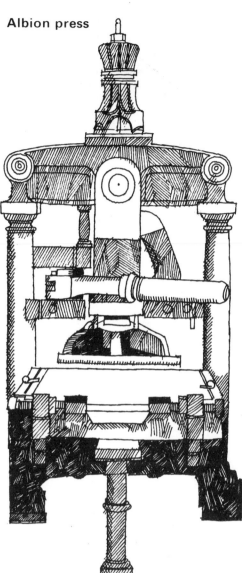

Albion press

If at all possible, try to use a press such as an *Albion* or a *mangle-type* etching press. These are to be found in most art schools, some art centres, and even in some schools. A heavier deposit of ink will give the print a sharper, more positive look.

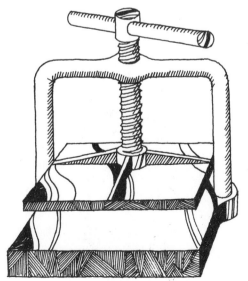

Pinch press

It is also possible, as card is composed of a number of sheets stuck together, to cut down into some of the layers like a bas-relief carving and this will create textural interest. Try cutting out large areas of card down to a certain depth, or gouge out small marks. If these are painted with shellac and allowed to dry, the result will be a block that is tough and resilient. This can be inked-up by covering the entire surface with ink, then wiping it off. The ink that remains in the hollows and cavities is the image which will print. This form of printing is called *intaglio*.

When printing, the printing paper has to be rubbed very hard to make the paper accept the ink from the different levels. (Intaglio block shown above.)

Another method that is simple to carry out is to cut the card into various shapes. Place the printing paper on top of the un-inked card. Hold the paper in position and pass a lightly inked roller over the top of the paper. This picks up the shapes under the paper. It is called a *roller rubbing* and is soft but definite in character.

It is also possible to glue shapes of card to a block as in the chapter on string prints. It is then printed in the same way. Try cutting the simple shape of a house or a face and glue these onto a base. Use pieces of various types of card, thick, thin, textured and patterned.

Try inking up some sections as in the jigsaw designs, to make mobiles to hang from the ceiling. Cut fish shapes or butterflies. Ink them up in bright colours and print them. Add details of scales or wing markings using other methods of printing. Attach them to a thread and hang them to float in space.

Try cutting your card into various shapes and see what ideas they suggest to you. Find an old jigsaw puzzle and make prints from it in different ways. Try merging different colours across each piece of the jigsaw.

Rubbings

Rubbings, also known by the French term *frottage* are a way of making prints that is familiar to most people. A sheet of thin soft paper is laid on top of a raised surface and then a pencil, crayon or roller is used to make an impression. The rubbing usually shows up particular aspects of the surface, giving it a different value. It is possible to make a rubbing from a three dimensional object by wrapping the printing paper around it and rubbing slowly all over the sheet. Rubbings taken from church brasses are very popular. Unfortunately, some of the most famous brasses are becoming badly worn away with too much rubbing.

For the process of rubbing itself, use wax or pastel crayons, soft pencils or cobbler's wax in any colours. As subjects for the rubbings, make a collection of flat objects that are in relief. Surfaces that are suitable for rubbing are available everywhere. Wooden floorboards, fabrics, brick walls, iron gratings, manhole covers, and textured areas can be found indoors and out.

The paper used should be tough, thin and white. A thin Japanese paper is good and some art shops stock paper which is specially prepared for rubbing.

Select the surface you are going to rub and place the paper on it. Holding it firmly with one hand, rub over the paper with a crayon that is held flat, as this makes for a sharper image.

It is best to clean the surface first by wiping it with a soft cloth to remove dirt and dust particles which could tear your paper.

If the subject is flat or can be laid on a table or on the floor, it is easiest to hold the paper in position with weights.

If the design does not seem to be showing up clearly, feel through the paper with the fingers and rub the surface.

If weights are not practical, sometimes the printing paper can be held in place with sticky tape, but the best type to use is *masking tape* from art stores or paint shops. This does not tear the paper when it is removed.

In many of the printing methods described in this book, such as potato cuts or lino cuts, the image prints in reverse. With rubbings, the image prints the same way round as the object the print is taken from, so it is possible to rub lettering and words from any raised surface.

Carved inscriptions and carved drawings lend themselves well to rubbing. A car incorporates so many aspects of lettering and decoration that it is possible to make many pictures from various parts, such as the radiator grill, the number plate, the door handles and the tyres. Mount your rubbings on cardboard and see how much of a car you can build up.

Rubbings taken from wood can be combined with rubbings from metal. Try taking a rubbing from your desk, especially if it is an old one with initials and names carved on it. Rub it sharply to preserve the clarity of the print.

Use the coins in your pocket, and a pencil. Rub both sides (the heads and the tails). Rub them in different colours on the same sheet of paper. Find a selection of coloured pencils and coloured crayons to use for rubbing, including a thick black wax crayon and a black carbon or graphite pencil. Try a soft graphite pencil or a ball point pen. All these should give different results from the same surfaces, so try them out on the coins and compare them.

Surface rolling, or roller rubbing, is produced by applying a roller charged with stiff ink, as described previously on p. 68. Start by getting together a few familiar household objects that will make a good rubbing, an engraved or impressed piece of kitchen equipment, the wooden handle of a bread knife with 'bread' written on it, or a collander. Take careful rubbings from these.

Take the rubbing materials out of doors and find inscriptions on buildings, lettering on lamp-posts, grids, walls, pavements, park benches and brass nameplates. Try making a survey of the different types of lettering found on nameplates. Make up a whole dictionary of categories like this.

Use old blocks that you have taken lino cuts or string prints from, and take rubbings using first a crayon or pencil and then a roller. Compare the results with the prints you took originally by the other methods.

Take rubbings of various kinds of wood. Find the knots and notice the differences in texture and grain which give the wood its character. Use weathered driftwood, old floor boards and new planks.

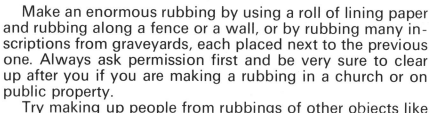

Make an enormous rubbing by using a roll of lining paper and rubbing along a fence or a wall, or by rubbing many inscriptions from graveyards, each placed next to the previous one. Always ask permission first and be very sure to clear up after you if you are making a rubbing in a church or on public property.

Try making up people from rubbings of other objects like knives, clothes, pegs and spoons.

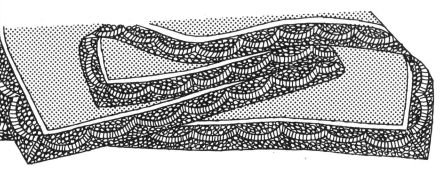

Think of varied and unusual objects and surfaces to take rubbings from, such as embroidery, lace, leaded windows, clothing or shoes.

Use a new colour for each separate rubbing on a sheet of paper. Try a second rubbing on top of an existing rubbing, making the second one much clearer.

Take rubbings from various three dimensional objects by wrapping the paper round the object and rubbing carefully, section by section. Try doing this with an embossed vase, a brogue shoe, a metal or plastic dustbin lid, a child's toy.

Reconstruct an object such as a brick by taking a rubbing from each of its six sides, mounting them on a card and sticking them together. Ask a friend to co-operate with you and see just how much of him and his clothes you can take a rubbing from. Start with the shoes and work up.

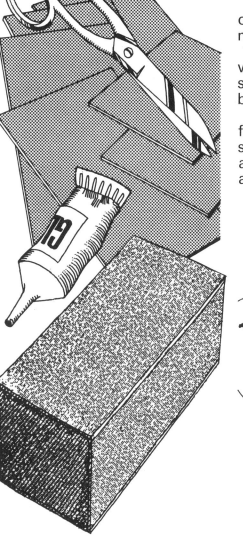

Make up pictures by using various subjects on the same sheet. Make up portraits of your parents by rubbing different objects to make up the features, fruit for faces and wool for hair. Clothing can be added from fabrics.

Now that you have read all about printmaking, develop your own ideas using the methods you like best. Printmaking is a hobby that could last a lifetime.

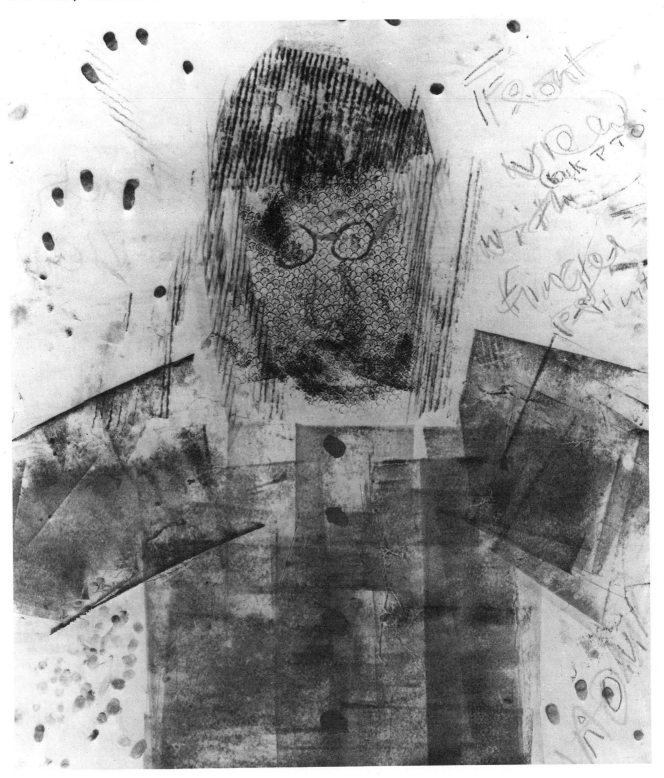

Glossary

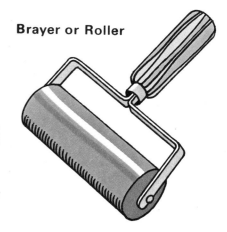

Blind Printing Printing from un-inked blocks or plates. The image is seen because it is raised into a 3 dimensional form.

Brayer or Roller Hand roller made in rubber, plastic or gelatine, for inking up blocks and plates.

Cardboard A smooth white board.

Collage Sticking material, paper, and other materials onto a background.

Collage

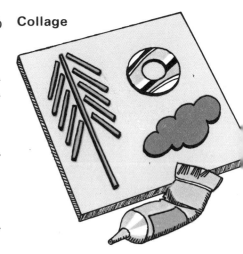

Embossing Also known as gauffrage or Kara-zuri. Printing from un-inked blocks or plates which give a 3 dimensional image. (See *Blind Printing*)

Frottage A print taken directly from surfaces by rubbing.

Glue Block A block made from thick glue on a base.

Gouache A painting medium: finely ground opaque water paint.

Heelball or **Cobbler's Wax** Hard wax used by shoe-menders; widely used for taking rubbings: can be bought at shoemenders.

Intaglio

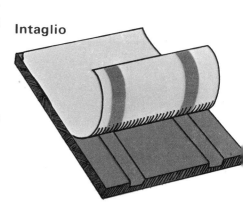

Impression A print in any media using any method.

Intaglio A print taken from indentations lower than the surface of the plate or block being printed.

Jig or Bench Hook Wooden device on which lino rests when cutting.

Key Block The master drawing or block, usually a line drawing, from which other blocks are made.

Jig or Bench Hook

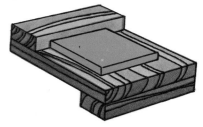

Key Drawing The master drawing (see *Registration*).

Lino Cut Linoleum gouged, cut and printed in relief.

Merge (see *Rainbow Printing*).

Monoprint A 'one off' print which cannot be repeated.

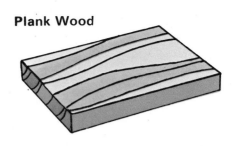

Plank Wood

Offset To transfer a design from one surface to another.

Plank Wood The material from which woodcuts are made; the grain runs across the surface of the block.

Planographic Printed from a flat surface (i.e. lithography, screen printing).

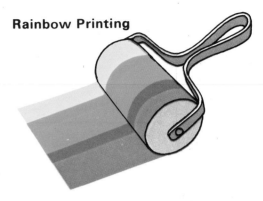

Rainbow Printing

Proof A print taken before the block or plate has been finished.

Proof Trial A print made by the artist to check on the development of the work.

Rainbow Printing or Merge Separate colours blended smoothly together with a roller and then rolled on a block.

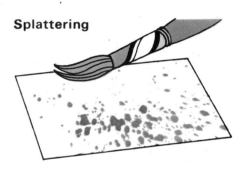

Splattering

Registration The accurate positioning of blocks and printing paper.

Relief Print A print taken from the top surface of any relief block.

Roller offset A print made with a composition roller. (See *Offset*.)

Stippling

Splattering Flicking ink onto a printing paper with a brush.

Stencil A perforated mask or stencil onto which ink is dabbed or painted so that the shapes of the perforations appear on the printing paper placed under the stencil.

Stippling Dabbing with a brush to make textured surface.

Transfer Drawing A print made by pressure on the back of paper placed lightly, face down, on an inked slab.

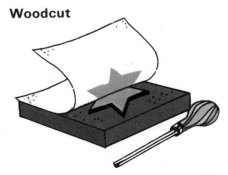

Woodcut

Transparent base Base to mix with ink or pigment in order to improve its transparency, e.g. wallpaper paste.

Woodcut Plank wood cut with gouges or knives, printed in relief.